The "Wallonien"

The History of the
5th SS-Sturmbrigade
and
28th SS Volunteer
Panzergrenadier Division

Richard Landwehr
Jean-Louis Roba
Ray Merriam

MERRIAM PRESS

Hoosick Falls, New York
2020

Originally published under the same title by
Weapons and Warfare Press in conjunction with
Siegrunen Magazine (Richard Landwehr) in 1984.

First published by the Merriam Press in 1988
(formerly known as International Graphics Corporation,
dba Weapons and Warfare Press, aka Weapons and Warfare Publications)

Sixth Edition (2020)

ISBN 978-1-716-46391-4

This work was designed, produced, and published in
the United States of America by the

Merriam Press
489 South Street
Hoosick Falls NY 12090

E-mail: ray@merriam-press.com
Web site: merriam-press.com

The Merriam Press has published numerous titles on historical subjects, especially military history, with an emphasis on World War II, as well as making available previously published works, including reports, documents, manuals, articles
and other materials on historical topics, some in printed form with many as PDF
files. Also the eBook magazine series *World War 2 in Review* and the pictorial PDF
series *World War 2 Album*.

Contents

The "Wallonien"

Chapter 1

Introduction

by Jean-Louis Roba and Ray Merriam

In 1944, Germany was on the defensive in every theater. On the Mediterranean Front, the Anglo-American forces had invaded southern Italy; in the East, the German Army was fighting the numerically superior Soviet Army.

The Soviets had the initiative and tried to trap the German divisions in pockets (ala Stalingrad); those pockets had to be reduced. At the beginning of the year, two such pockets were created: one at Korsun (Tcherkassy) in February, another in the area of Kamenets-Podolsk in March. In the former there was a unit of foreign volunteers: the 5th SS Freiwilligen Sturmbrigade "Wallonien."

The brigade was created by the Rexist Party, founded by Leon Degrelle, a Belgian lawyer born at Bouillon. He was the leader of one of the numerous "fascist" parties which existed before the outbreak of World War II. His purpose was actually historic: to make a great Burgundy with the southern part of Belgium and a part of northern France. His dream: to recreate the duchy of Charles the Bold before his death at Nancy in 1477 (the Kings of France [17th and 18th centuries] conquered some portions of ancient Burgundy and made them a part of their kingdom).

Degrelle, who was emphatic (and in the opinion of his men sometimes boring), was also a politician: he collaborated with the German occupation forces. But when "Unternehmen Barbarossa" began, he enlisted in the Wehrmacht. Cleverly, he understood that if Germany won the war, Hitler would give benefits to people who were ready to give their lives for the German cause.

Degrelle enlisted in the Heer, accepting a commission as an officer and tried to gain the confidence of the German High Command.[1]

The Germans were impressed with the fighting capabilities of the Walloon soldiers in the southern sector of the Russian front. It is difficult to describe the men who formed the Walloon unit; some were naturally members of the Rexist Party but others volunteered for numerous other reasons. There were soldiers of the Belgian Army who wanted to avenge the defeat of 1940 and provide Belgium with some honor; some wanted to fight the "Reds." Some went to provide for their family or to be far from the Belgian tribunals.[2]

In 1943 the Waffen-SS needed new 'blood' after the terrible battles in the East. In June, the Walloon volunteers were handed over to the Waffen-SS and the unit was designated "5.SS Freiwilligen Sturmbrigade Wallonien." An unusual characteristic of this Sturmbrigade was its "padre," truly uncommon in the "pagan SS," but the Rexist Party was a Christian one and Degrelle wanted to maintain the "traditions."

The new Sturmbrigade fought on the Dnieper bend and was trapped in the Korsun pocket with another foreign unit of the Waffen-SS, the famed 5th SS Panzer Division "Wiking."[3] The military commander of the unit, Obersturmbannführer Lucien Lippert, was killed at Nowo-Buda on 15 February 1944.[4] His death left Hauptsturmführer Degrelle in command. The Walloons escaped from the pocket with 632 men of the approximately 2,000 who were trapped in the "Kessel."[5] The courage of the Walloons

---

[1] Flemish men who desired to fight on the Eastern Front had to join the Waffen-SS—an intentional segregation whose intent was to divide Belgium's populace.

[2] One soldier went to the Eastern Front to get away from his woman, a terrible shrew. He lost an arm in the battle of the Korsun Pocket.

[3] In order to save German troops, the Oberkommando sent foreign volunteer units to all the "hot spots." This practice provided the Walloon soldiers with numerous honors near the village of Tcherkassy … and very heavy losses.

[4] Lippert was an officer of the Belgian Army who wanted to participate in the "crusade against Bolshevism."

[5] In the first days of the battle, a number of Walloons were evacuated by air, so losses were approximately fifty per cent.

The "Wallonien"

so impressed the other units that when the exhausted men of the Wehrmacht and the "Wiking" (who escaped from the pocket) saw the hastily-made coffin of Lippert carried by four of his men, they jumped to their feet to salute the corpse of the fallen officer. The Walloons did not want to leave the body of the Obersturmbannführer to the Soviets.

As soon as the battle ended, Degrelle was ordered to the Führerhauptquartier. He left for Uman in a Fieseler Fi 156 where a special plane for Degrelle, Gen. der Wehrmacht Liebe and "Wiking" Division Commander Gruppenführer SS Herbert Otto Gille was waiting. The Walloon and his two superiors were received by the Führer who presented the Knight's Cross to Degrelle and the Swords of the Knight's Cross to Gille.

Naturally, the German propaganda media did its best to propagate the news. Germany needed more men to face the Soviet advance and the occupied countries could provide those soldiers. After his visit to Hitler, Degrelle went to Paris where he spoke before ten thousand collaborators at the Palais de Chaillot. The Battle of Tcherkassy had a great impact on Belgian opinion. It would not be an exaggeration to compare it to the Battle of Bir Hakeim; that was the first great action of the Free French troops and gave confidence to the partisans of De Gaulle. And the circumstances were nearly the same. In both cases, men of a volunteer unit in a foreign army were encircled by superior forces. They fought under terrible climatic conditions (desert versus winter) and distinguished themselves. They broke through the encirclement and managed to get back to their lines. In both cases, there was no victory, only a glorious escape.

But, for the Germans, it was too late. Four months later the Allies landed in Normandy.

The example of the "Wallonien" enthused not only the Belgian collaborators, but also a portion of the French population. Every young man who enlisted in the 33rd Waffen-SS Grenadier Division "Charlemagne" hoped to equal the reputation of the Walloon "comrades." And the story of Tcherkassy, as described by Goebbel's services, brought new recruits to the SS.

After his speech at Paris, Degrelle rejoined his men at Vlodawa in Poland. The new commander had asked to have some rest and the depleted brigade had to make triumphal parades in its homeland. It was also done for propaganda purposes: the Soviet High Command had said that all the units trapped in Korsun had been destroyed, "... the brigade of Walloon traitors included."

Via Wildflecken, the Sturmbrigade went to Beverloo in Belgium. Beverloo has great barracks well-known in the Belgian Army. At that time, the Oberkommando had made it the formation center of another SS unit: the 12th SS Panzer Division "Hitler Jugend."[6] Since the Brigade had lost many men and all their material, the "Hitler Jugend" lent some vehicles and soldiers to provide more depth for the parades.

The first town which received a visit from the unit was Charleroi on 1 April 1944, being the fifth city of Belgium and the third of Wallony; it was supposed to have provided the most courageous men of the Brigade. The parade occurred in the center of the town, on the "Place Charles II," and there were many personalities present: Oberbefehlshaber für Belgien und Nordfrankreich Raeder and the Commander of the 1st SS Panzer Division "Leibstandarte Adolf Hitler," Oberstgruppenführer "Sepp" Dietrich.[7] Gruppenführer Jungclauss, Himmler's representative in Belgium, was also present.

---

[6] It was the habit of the Germans to raise and train new units in the occupied countries. For instance, also trained in Belgium, in 1942, the 65th Infantry Division (in the Antwerp-Turnhout area) and, in 1943, the 44th Infantry Division "Hoch und Deutschmeister" (in the Ghent-Bruges area).

[7] It is a little surprising to see Dietrich in Belgium but his division was trapped in the Kamenets-Podolsk Pocket with the remnants of the 1st Panzer Army. Saved by the 2nd SS Panzerkorps, the unit was sent to the West for rest and refitting. Being in Belgium, it was an excellent opportunity to honor the Walloon volunteers with the presence of one of the "old fighters" of the Nazi regime. There were some links between the LAH and HJ divisions. Indeed, when it was decided to make a new division with young boys from the Hitler Youth, the commander was quickly found: Fritz Witt, one of the best officers of the LAH. Sepp Dietrich was enthused with the idea to create a "young LAH" and provided Witt with all the officers he wanted. The new commander chose three of the best: Obersturmbannführer Kurt Meyer (better known as "Panzermeyer"), Obersturmbannführer Wilhelm Mohnke and Sturmbannführer Max Wuensche, a blond warrior in his black Panzer uniform, future leader of the armored regiment of the "Baby Division" (as the Allied troops named it). Thus, it is not too

continued...

A Luftwaffe band was on the square and played the "Braban-conne" (Belgian national anthem) and the "Vers l'Avenir" (Rexist Party song). Seventy-five men of the Wallonien were presented with the Iron Cross.

After the ceremony at Charleroi, the column proceeded to Brussels. The trucks and vehicles had to maintain a distance of fifty meters between them. At that time the Allied fighter-bombers were making frequent sweeps over the country and attacked anything moving on the roads. Some flak vehicles were in the column but it was not enough to provide complete protection.

At Brussels the second parade took place. The Wallonien crossed the town from south to north. The vehicles defiled in front of the "Bourse" (the Belgian stock exchange building). Degrelle was in his Sd.Kfz. 251 half-track with his children by his side, wanting to show them the parade. As at Charleroi, all the pro-German authorities were present and saluted the survivors of the Sturmbrigade.

At the end of the day, all was over: the vehicles and the men of the "Hitler Jugend" went back to Beverloo; the Walloons had a short three weeks rest at home near their families. After that period, they were sent, with new recruits, to Estonia. There, as well as in Pomerania, they engaged in fierce battles. The unit met its end on the shores of the Baltic Sea. Degrelle managed to escape to Norway and fly to Spain (where he still resides as of this writing).

Of all the officers of high rank who were standing on the steps of the town hall of Charleroi only two are living as of this writing: Degrelle and Wuensche.[8]

...*continued*

surprising to find the four men (Witt, Meyer, Mohnke and Wuensche) present at Charleroi. They came for three reasons: 1) to see again their "old Dietrich" and their comrades of the LAH; 2) to honor the good soldiers of the Sturmbrigade Wallonien; 3) to keep an eye on the men and materiel they lent to the Wallonien (we must not forget the terrible shortage of soldiers and vehicles in 1944).

[8] Witt died in Normandy 16 June 1944; Meyer in 1965; Dietrich in 1967.

SOURCES

Degrelle, Leon. *La campagnede Russie.*

Fraschka, Guenther. *L'Honneur n 'a pas de Frontieres.*

"L'Internationale SS." *Historia Magazine.*

Landemer, Henri. *Les Waffen-SS.*

Mabire, Jean. *Les Jeunes Fauves du Fuehrer.*

Stein, George. *The Waffen-SS.*

Terlin, Paul. *La Neige et le Sang.*

Windrow, Martin, and Michael Roffe. *Waffen-SS.*

Chapter 2

Formation and First Engagements of the 5th SS-Sturmbrigade "Wallonien"

O n 1 June 1943, the Legion "Wallonie" was transferred into the Waffen-SS from the German Army and given the title SS-Freiwilligen-Brigade "Wallonien." The Legion "Wallonie" had originally been recruited by the Waffen-SS in 1941 only to be turned over to the Wehrmacht later in the autumn of 1941 when the SS High Command decided that the Walloons were not sufficiently "Germanic" to qualify for Waffen-SS status. By 1943 all of this had changed thanks mainly to two things:

1) The incredible performance of the battalion-sized Legion on the southern sector of the Eastern Front in 1942, and,

2) Leon Degrelle, the dynamic Belgian political leader who had risen through the ranks in the Legion from private to lieutenant. Degrelle's brilliant personal performance was not lost on either Reichsführer-SS Himmler or Adolf Hitler, and as a result he was able to convince them that the Legion "Wallonie" really belonged in the elite Waffen-SS

In June 1943 the formation of the "Wallonien" SS Brigade got underway at the Pieske training camp near Meseritz, using as its base some 1,600 veterans of the "Legion" and the Belgian Army, along with another 400 fresh recruits from Belgium. The commander was a former Belgian Army general staff officer named Lucien Lippert, who was given the rank of SS-Obersturmbannführer (lieutenant colonel).

Lippert was 29 years old and had graduated as the best in his class at the military academia in Brussels. He was an idealist with a truly knightly bearing. His second-in-command was SS--

Hauptsturmführer Leon Degrelle, who was also in charge of one of the infantry companies. About two-thirds of the "Wallonien" Brigade was composed of young workers, craftsmen, and the sons of industrialists, diplomats and civic leaders along with many highly regarded students from colleges and Jesuit schools. The rest of the personnel were primarily ex-Belgian Army soldiers.

The new brigade received inspection visits from RF-SS Himmler on 16 and 24 June, and as a consequence, it was transferred to the better equipped training camp at Wildflecken (Rhoen). On 3 July 1943 the unit was upgraded to the SS-Sturmbrigade (Assault Brigade) "Wallonien."

From July to October, the Sturmbrigade was kept busy with continuous training exercises. During this period of time the unit had the following internal structure:

- Staff and Administrative Services
- 1st through 3rd Companies (Infantry)
- 4th and 5th Companies (Heavy Weapons) [5th Company may not have been deployed at this time]
- Replacement Company
- 1st Assault Gun Battery [added late in 1943]
- Motorcycle Platoon
- Engineer Platoon
- Five Heavy Weapons Platoons [presumably attached to each of the Infantry Companies]
- One Motorized Transport Column

During the summer and autumn of 1943, the Walloon officer candidates were sent to the SS Junkerschule (Officer's School) Tölz while NCO prospects were dispatched to the SS NCO School at Posen-Treskau. The anti-tank troops were trained at Ayrs, East Prussia with the infantry gun (light field artillery) crews being sent to Breslau-Lissa. Engineer troops were dispatched to the SS Combat Engineer School at Dresden with communications elements going to the SS Signals School in Nuremberg. The infantrymen remained at Wildflecken where they were rejoined by the heavy weapons sections in late October at which time joint unit exercises were carried out.

During the first part of November 1943, the SS Sturmbrigade "Wallonien" was rushed to the Titonir-Bielaye-Tserkom sector in

Ukraine on the lower Dnieper where large Soviet forces were threatening the German defenders with encirclement. "Wallonien" arrived in Ukraine on 11 November 1943 and was assigned to the 5th SS Panzer Division "Wiking" as a reinforcement. At the time, "Wiking" was attempting to contain Soviet infiltrations through the marshy forests of the Olschanka-Smela front. Traveling via Lviv-Jassy-Kitchinev, the Walloons arrived at the Korsun railroad in six troop trains on the night of 19/20 November. Here the Sturmbrigade was placed under the charge of SS-Gruppenführer (lieutenant general) Herbert-Otto Gille, commander of the "Wiking" Division.

By 26 November, "Wallonien" was in position on a twenty kilometer front along the Olschanka River. Second Company was kept in reserve at Smela until 6 December 1943. At this time the Sturmbrigade strength stood as follows: thirty-eight officers, 219 NCOs, 1,715 men. Total: 1,972 personnel. There were 250 motorized vehicles, forty-six artillery pieces and eighteen heavy mortars assigned to the unit.

The Sturmbrigade sent out its first reconnaissance patrols during the first part of December. These parties were plagued by heavy snows in the forests and swamps and by enemy ambushes. On 13 December a patrol led by SS-Obersturmführer (first lieutenant) Van Esden was surprised by female communist troops. In the lop-sided fight that followed, eighteen of the twenty Walloons in the patrol were killed. On 22 December, 3rd Company made heavy contact with the enemy near Jrdin.

During this time the "Wallonien" frontlines were tightened up and by early in December stretched for only about seven kilometers near the edge of the great Cherkassy Forest. Twelve heavy machine guns and four heavy mortars were placed in or near the forward positions. The "Wallonien" was also responsible for protecting a large wooden bridge over the Olschanka from enemy air attack and from time to time a Soviet plane was shot down by some of the Walloon light Flak gunners.

The general military situation was not good; the Soviets had pushed the German lines back at Kirovograd shortly before Christmas, and the weather had gotten quite cold with low temperatures down to minus 25 degrees Centigrade during the nights. As the new year came, the "Wallonien" front sector on the Olschanka from Losovok to Starosselje was ominously quiet, and it was felt that the Reds were preparing for a major assault. To counteract this, the Sturmbrigade planned a preventative attack on Soviet fortifications near the village of Sakrefka. The "Wallonien" effort involved three infantry companies, the engineer platoon and the assault gun battery. The attack got underway on 4 January as elements of the "Wallonien" closed in on Sakrefka from three different directions. One infantry company was ferried across the Olschanka in rubber boats by the engineers, while another company rode into battle on the assault guns and the third company attacked on foot.

The Soviets were fully taken by surprise. Their anti-tank gunners were not even able to load their weapons before they were overrun by the assault guns. Only the 3rd Company had any serious difficulties. Some of the enemy soldiers woke up in time to fire some of their heavy weapons at this company. But other than that it was largely a rout. There was one memorable "Wild West" incident when the Walloon officer Untersturmführer (second lieutenant) Albert Robin engaged a Soviet captain in a pistol showdown. Robin won the duel by getting his shot off first. Considered a real daredevil, Robin went on to lead 125 attacks in the "Cherkassy Pocket" struggle without even getting wounded.

The Walloons found that the Soviet officers fought bravely at Sakrefka, but such was not the case for many of the privates, who were mostly Asiatics. The volunteers who had served in the old Legion "Wallonie" in 1941-42, were fascinated by the new, more decorative officer's uniforms with their shining shoulder straps. This was part of Stalin's temporary wartime scheme to restore more power and authority to the officer's corps at the expense of the political authorities. In the process certain practices from the old "Imperial" Army were reintroduced only to be rescinded again after the war ended. One of the Walloon volunteers remarked (after viewing captive officers): "Before we only fought against Bolshevism—now we must fight Holy Russia!"

The successful battle at Sakrefka helped restore the confidence of the "Wallonien" soldiers, but the fear of encirclement was already present. The rumor circulated through the Brigade on 9 January that the Soviets had succeeded in surrounding them, but the staff immediately denied this piece of misinformation. Still, it remained in the back of everyone's minds. On 10 January, retreat orders were given to the "Wallonien" units because enemy tanks had reached the Bug River and there was nothing left to stop them with. Towards the end of the day, with the companies engaged in loading up their trucks with supplies and equipment, new orders arrived from the "Wiking" Division: "The Sturmbrigade must remain at Mochny; no retreat for the moment." This was quite a disappointment for the Walloons in the frontlines, but four days later they were relieved by the Estonian SS Battalion "Narva" and were sent back to the Teclino Forest.

There was a Red Army enclave in the Teclino Forest that needed to be eliminated and Gruf. Gille chose the "Wallonien" to do the job. At 0400 on 15 January, the long-range guns of 4th Company began to bombard the enemy positions. They fired some 4,000 shells and were able to obliterate the first Soviet line of defense. After that the three "Wallonien" infantry companies moved in. During the early part of the battle the Soviets were still stunned from the artillery bombardment and they quickly began to fall back.

After covering about 500 to 600 meters, the Belgian volunteers began to run into stiffer resistance. In the 2nd Company (which had a lot of Belgian Army ex-POWs in its ranks), one soldier was observed replacing his helmet with a Royal Belgian Army field cap, but he was killed shortly thereafter. Many of the Soviet opponents proved to be women with their heads' shaved. They fired submachine guns and put up a terrible resistance. The 3rd Company had to assault one of these "Amazon" positions three times before finally conquering it.

Finally the Soviet artillery began to shoot back and in thirty minutes of carnage, the attacking Sturmbrigade lost two hundred men. Many of them were to die on their way back to Mochny. When that bombardment subsided, the Reds counterattacked. The Walloons soon lost much of the ground that they had gained and were almost pushed back to their jumping-off points. Third Company, which was composed for the most part of very young soldiers, stayed in place in the forest and refused to retreat.

In the meantime the twelve heavy machine guns of 4th Company continued to shoot without pause. The Soviets continued their counterattack without cover and as a result suffered heavy losses. Their corpses were soon piled high before the main "Wallonien" defensive lines. Finally the men of the Sturmbrigade launched a wild bayonet charge against the Soviets. In a short but hectic struggle the first enemy defensive lines were again retaken, but six more Walloons died in the fighting.

The SS volunteers dug in for a hard, cold night. Frostbite was common and, in fact, anyone that fell asleep stood a good chance of freezing to death. On 16 January some brave souls brought up supplies to the new frontlines and the Walloons built wooden bunkers and dug in to wait for another enemy attack. Fortunately the Soviets never came back so this turned out to be a day of rest. In the early morning hours of 17 January assault troops were sent out to explore the enemy defenses. Many of the foremost scouts never returned; they were probably the victims of Soviet mines.

The Walloon raiding parties managed to slip into the enemy defensive system and at 0500 hours the order was passed on to attack. Simultaneously, the other Sturmbrigade companies also began their assault and the Reds soon found themselves being hit from the rear and the front. By 1200 hours the main fighting was all over except for isolated pockets of resistance. During the early afternoon a platoon of forty Mongols refused to surrender so they had to be eliminated to the last man.

By 18 January 1944, the men of the "Wallonien" had taken some six hundred enemy bunkers, but skirmishing continued to the next day. The price of defeat was graphically revealed when the bodies of a Danish SS man who had been "crucified" and an Estonian SS man who had been horribly tortured to death were found. More proof, if any more was needed, as to the primal bestiality of the foe.

Soon afterwards the "Wallonien" reassembled at Belloserje, where the headquarters of the "Wiking" Division was located.

The survivors of the Sturmbrigade were tired but in a jubilant mood; they had "proved" themselves. Gruppenführer Gille had wanted to see if "his" Walloons could fight and they had certainly done that. Now Gille personally inspected the "Wallonien," stopping before each man to shake his hand and take his picture. At his side was the Sturmbrigade commanding officer, Ostubaf. Lippert. After the distribution of some Iron Crosses, Hstuf. Degrelle gave a short speech in German to the "Wallonien." Since Degrelle's German was not all that fluent at the time, Gruf. Gille had some difficulty keeping a straight face throughout the address.

Chapter 3

The Cherkassy-Korsun Envelopment

On 28 January 1944, the "Wallonien" Brigade, the "Wiking" Division and five other German divisions at various levels of strength, found themselves suddenly encircled when Soviet spearheads linked up some eighty kilometers to their rear. Thus began one of the most dramatic struggles for survival by trapped forces to take place in World War II. Specifically, the cut off German units consisted of the following:

- XLII Army Corps under General Lieb with the following divisions:
  - 88th Infantry
  - 5th SS Panzer Division "Wiking" (to which the "Wallonien" Brigade was attached)
- Corps Detachment B (consisting of the bulk of 112th Infantry Division plus the remnants of two other divisions)
- XI Army Corps under General Stemmermann with the following divisions:
  - 57th Infantry Division
  - 72nd Infantry Division
  - 389th Infantry Division
- One independent assault gun brigade with six batteries
- One detachment of light field artillery

A further evaluation of the trapped elements looked like this:

- 88th Infantry Division consisted of only five infantry battalions organized in two understrength regiments along with a weak artillery regiment.
- Corps Detachment B was the equivalent of a good infantry division.

- 5th SS Division "Wiking" was still in good shape with 7,000 troops organized into two panzergrenadier regiments, one artillery regiment and one panzer detachment (battalion size). It was further supplemented by the Estonian Volunteer Battalion "Narva."
- 5th SS Sturmbrigade "Wallonien" still had some 1,200 or so troops. Both "Wallonien" and "Wiking" had contingents outside of the entrapment.
- 72nd Infantry Division was still fully combat fit.
- 57th Infantry Division was very weak except for one good regiment.
- 389th Infantry Division was described as a "shadow of its former self."

Efforts at relieving the pocket began on 29 January, with the two Corps inside of the encirclement authorized to shift their forces so as to best prepare for an eventual escape. This meant that a withdrawal of the northern and eastern pocket units had to be carried out to bolster the southern part of the envelopment. Also on this day, air re-supply and the evacuation of wounded began at Korsun airfield. In the course of the encirclement battle, 2,188 wounded soldiers would be safely airlifted out, but a few hundred others would die when their medical evacuation planes were shot down and an unknown number of wounded captured by the Soviets were simply put to death.

The "Wallonien" Brigade defended positions on the extreme eastern corner of the cauldron and received the brunt of the initial enemy attacks. When the shooting let up the Walloons were surprised to hear a loudspeaker broadcasting to them. The speaker was a man who spoke French with a Parisian accent and he gave the Walloons a message of gloom and despair pertaining to their present plight, ending up by urging them to surrender or desert. About fifty members of the Sturmbrigade had either deserted or been captured up to this point, so the Soviets had gotten a pretty good rundown about "Wallonien" and its defensive positions from them.

The first major battle for the "Wallonien" sector broke out during the night of 1/2 February. At 0800 on 2 February, Soviet troops assaulted the eastern-most portion of the Sturmbrigade lines between Losovok and the Dnieper River. The two dozen

The "Wallonien"

Walloon defenders in the area were overrun. A little bit later in the morning the "Wallonien" headquarters at Losovok was forced to pull out and the town was lost. With the help of tanks and artillery from the "Wiking" Division, 2nd Company launched a prompt counterattack. In very bitter hand-to-hand fighting Losovok was retaken, but towards the end of the day, the "Wallonien" was ordered to evacuate its defensive sector, so the hard-won gains proved to have been in vain.

The Sturmbrigade was to pull back to a depth of twenty kilometers from its old positions around Mochny. This was easier said than done, since the transport trucks and supply vehicles had a difficult time moving on the very muddy makeshift roads. In the course of the withdrawal many of the isolated "Wallonien" outposts got separated and it was important to see that they regrouped at Belloserje by 3 February. To try and round up all of the straggling elements, Hstuf. Degrelle drove off through the swamps in his VW command car, accompanied only by a single soldier. In the course of a hair-raising journey, Degrelle passed behind some enemy forces and was nearly captured by a Soviet patrol in an otherwise deserted village. In the end he got back safely to the German lines.

The new "Wallonien" front ran for a length of thirty kilometers from Starosselje to a point behind Derenkowetz. It was clear that this much territory could not be held for long by the depleted Belgian brigade and in fact, during the night of 3/4 February, substantial communist partisan elements infiltrated the lines and slipped through into the woods to the west of the "Wallonien" positions. They immediately blocked off the remaining roads to the west, which left the Walloons with the only option of continuing to withdraw along the Starosselje road to the south.

On 4 February, "Wallonien" was supposed to occupy some positions between Starosselje and Derenkowetz that had been built by Ukrainian laborers the previous January. But getting there was a tough assignment; the roads seemed to be composed of near bottomless mud and many vehicles got continually stuck and took hours to extricate. In addition, hundreds of Ukrainian women and children along with their livestock, had decided to join the retreat, thus congesting the traffic problems even more.

When the Sturmbrigade finally got into its new lines on 5 February, the three hundred or so survivors from the three infantry companies were spread very thinly along the front, with the other "Wallonien" members placed into supporting positions to their rear. As yet, there were no particular re-supply problems, as adequate amounts of ammunition were flown into Korsun each day and there were plenty of rations due to the fact that the civil authorities had used some foresight for a change and had managed to shift the contents from supply depots east of the Dnieper to Korsun well ahead of the enemy advance.

The new "Wallonien" lines proved to be completely untenable. Just prior to dawn on 6 February the enemy broke through in force, and the Sturmbrigade was soon fighting for survival. In wild and violent close-combat the Walloons were able to make their way to the safety of high ground by late in the afternoon, while some platoons managed to hold onto Starosselje and Derenkowetz. Fighting continued to rage throughout the next two days. On 8 February the central "Wallonien" positions near Skiti were lost then retaken in a particularly savage engagement.

To coordinate the breakout from the pocket, Gen. Stemmermann was named to command all of the trapped German forces on 7 February. It was his job to coordinate an attack from inside the encirclement with attacks to be launched from the outside by XLVIII Panzer Corps to the south and III Panzer Corps to the southwest. Stemmermann had developed his final breakout plans by 10 February, but they had to be continually postponed due to the weather conditions and the slow progress by the outside forces. At a bare minimum it was necessary for III Panzer Corps to capture the town of Lisyanka to establish some sort of escape corridor, providing that the trapped German units could punctuate the pocket near that point. Fortunately, III Panzer Corps would be able to take Lisyanka, but could do little more than that.

In the meantime, on 9 February, the entire pocket was in motion towards the west and the lives of some fifty thousand soldiers hung in the balance. "Wallonien" spent the day fighting for every step of the way along the eastern edge of the encirclement. In the afternoon most of the Sturmbrigade transport column was shot up by enemy tanks and more than one hundred trucks were destroyed and all the unit's records were lost. The drivers were now formed into a combat reserve. The "Wallonien" light artillery gunners and infantrymen would manage to defend a bridgehead around Derenkowetz through the morning of 11 February. At

1100 hours on that day, a Soviet delegation approached the "Wallonien" positions under a white flag and handed over a surrender ultimatum for the Corps' commander. They brought with them letters from captured German generals who had joined up with the Reds. Such efforts were being made all along the front to secure an easy surrender; it later turned out that the Soviets had seriously overestimated the German strength in the pocket. However, all capitulation ultimatums were categorically rejected and the couriers were sent packing.

By 13 February, "Wallonien" reached the town of NovoBuda, but lost its last three armored vehicles while getting there. The next day the Walloons had to defend the town against continuous enemy assaults. While leading his troops in close combat in the center of Novo-Buda, Ostubaf. Lippert was killed by an explosive shell. Hauptsturmführer Degrelle then took charge of the brigade and for the next few days would lead it in continuous defensive actions around the town. He would twice be grazed by bullets and also have a shell fragment pierce his coat and lodge between it and his shirt. A wounded Obersturmführer and two volunteers took charge of Ostubaf. Lippert's body; they would not let it fall into the hands of the Reds. In the end they would swim it out of the pocket over a fast-flowing stream under enemy fire.

Now the real drama of the breakout began. On 28 January, the pocket had been as big in width and depth as the entire country of Belgium, but by 15 February it was so truncated and narrow that the enemy could fire completely across it from any side.

On 15 February, Gen. Lieb, the commander of XLII Corps, wrote the following extract in his diary:

> Our pocket is now so small that I can practically look over the entire front from my command post, when it is not snowing. Enemy aircraft are hard at work; lucky for us it is snowing most of the time. I was once more at Khilki to reconnoiter the terrain selected for the breakout. Then [I] issued the final orders. Since this morning there is trouble at the SS Division. The Walloons and the "Germania" Regiment are getting fidgety. They must hold only until tomorrow night.
>
> Final instructions from Stemmermann: We are to jump off on 16 February at 2300, with Corps Detachment N,

72nd Division and SS Panzer Division "Wiking" from Khilki-Komarovka across the line Dzhurzhentsy–Hill 239 to Lisyanka; 57th and 88th Divisions will cover the flanks and the rear.

With me, at my command post, are the three division commanders with whom I am supposed to perform this miracle tomorrow. One of them is doing this for the first time, the two others are old hands.

I left no doubt in their minds that, in my opinion, this is going to be one great mess, and that they should not get rattled no matter what happens. You need a guardian angel to bring you through this kind of thing.

On 16 February there was an aerial ammunition drop to the pocket which gave the trapped soldiers all that they would need for the breakout attempt. General Lieb made the hard decision to hand over some two thousand wounded, along with the medical personnel taking care of them, to the Russians. Since the Korsun airfield had been lost there was no longer any possibility for air evacuation. But despite orders to the contrary, most of the "pocket" units tried to take their wounded out along with them.

The breakout operation began at 2000 hours on the night of 16 February, finally getting in motion by 2300. At first everything started off in a well-organized manner, but when dawn broke and visibility improved the enemy caught on to what was happening and all hell broke loose. The main sticking point was that III Panzer Corps had not been able to take Hill 239 on the outskirts of the pocket as planned. This high ground remained in the hands of Soviet tank forces and this information was not passed on to the troops inside of the encirclement for fear that it would demoralize them. III Panzer Corps was only able to hold onto a small bottleneck into the enemy lines at Lisyank—this would be the only escape route available for "Force Stemmermann."

Throughout 17 February and into the morning of 18 February, the increasingly disassembled German units inside the pocket carried out numerous wild and desperate breakout attacks, that for the most part, worked. But after getting through the enemy-held high ground, one more obstacle to freedom was encountered: a nasty little river called the Gniloy Tikich, which was some thirty to fifty feet across and filled with ten feet of icy, rushing water. All

The "Wallonien"

too many soldiers lost their lives trying to get across it, and this insidious stream also claimed all of the remaining vehicles and heavy equipment of the escaping forces.

But other than that, the breakout was a passable success from the point of view of lives saved. Of the 56,000 soldiers originally encircled, all but 18,800 made it out of the pocket. However, through the magic of creative propaganda construction, the Soviets were able to come up with a different slate of figures altogether. According to them, the German losses stood at 55,000 killed and 18,000 captured, the sum total of which equaled some 17,000 more men than were ever in the encirclement. General Stemmermann was unfortunately killed in the breakout.

Hauptsturmführer Leon Degrelle managed to lead the survivors of the "Wallonien" Brigade, 632 in sum total, safely out of the entrapment along with 2,400 other soldiers and civilians that had been picked up en route. It was an amazing feat, not the least of which because the "Wallonien" Brigade had been the rear guard element for the whole engagement and was the last unit to make it out intact. Degrelle richly deserved the Knight's Cross award that was subsequently bestowed upon him.

Command Roster of the
5th SS Sturmbrigade "Wallonie"
January 1944

- **Commander:** Stubaf. Lucien Lippert (KIA)
- **Chief-of-Staff:** Hstuf. Francois Anthonissen (KIA)
- **German Liaison Officer:** Ostubaf. Wegener
- **Intelligence Officer:** Ostuf. Forteneicher
- **Ordnance Officer:** Hstuf. Leon Degrelle
- **Chaplain:** Abbe Fierens
- **Medical Service:** Hstuf. Dr. Schultz
- **Medical Service:** Dr. Stahl
- **Medical Service:** Dr. Lejeune
- **German Operations Officer:** Ostuf. Hans Drexel
- **Ukrainian SS Volunteer Platoon:** Waffen-Ostuf. Zawad sky
- **Motorcycle Recce Platoon:** Oscha. Deravot and Ostuf. Ronier
- **Engineer Platoon:** Ostuf. Mirgain
- **Signals Platoon:** Oscha. Lantiez
- **1st Grenadier Company:** Ostuf. Jules Mathieu
- **Adjutant:** Ustuf. Hubert Van Eyser (K IA)
- **2nd Grenadier Company:** Ostuf. Henri Derrickx
- **Adjutant:** Ustuf. Albert Wehinger
- **3rd Grenadier Company:** Ostuf. Robert Denie (previous commanding officer was Ostuf. Leon Degrelle)
- **Adjutant:** Oscha. Mueller (KIA)
- **4th Heavy Company (mortars and machine guns):** Ostuf. Marcel Bonniver
- **Adjutant:** Ustuf. Nicholas Zavadsky (KIA)
- **5th Anti-tank Company:** Ostuf. Marcel Lam proye
- **Adjutant:** Ustuf. Francois Daras (KIA)
- **6th Light Flak Company:** Ostuf. Louis Calonne
- **Adjutant:** Ustuf. Henri Thyssens (KIA)
- **7th Heavy Flak Company (88-mm guns):** Ostuf. Joseph Dumont
- **Adjutant:** Ustuf. Fernand Foulon
- **8th Battery (infantry guns):** Ostuf. Josy Graff
- **9th Battery (assault guns):** Ostuf. Pierre Dengis
- **10th Company (supply and transport):** Ostuf. Georges Ruelle

Chapter 4

"Wallonien" in Estonia

Following Cherkassy-Korsun and the homecoming parades in Belgium, 5th SS Sturmbrigade "Wallonien" returned to the Wildflecken Troop Training Grounds for another round of refitting. At this time (Spring 1944) the unit was restructured as follows:

- Brigade Staff
- I Battalion with 1st-4th Companies
- II Battalion with 5th-8th Companies
- Infantry Gun (Light Artillery) Company
- Anti-tank Company
- 1st and 2nd Flak (Air Defense) Companies
- Field Replacement (Reserve) Company

As of 30 June 1944, "Wallonien" had climbed back to the following strength totals: Fifty-three officers, 232 NCOs, 903 men for a total of 1,188 troops. The authorized strength was around 2,500 men.

At the end of July 1944, "Wallonien" received emergency directives to prepare a battalion for combat duty on the hardpressed Narva Front. Sturmbannführer Degrelle selected his I Battalion for the assignment and added part of the anti-tank company to it. Degrelle personally took charge of the small task force which totaled some 450 to 500 men. The battalion was first sent to guard the northern Estonian coastline on the Gulf of Finland, behind the "Tannenberg Positions" of the Narva Front. But in the middle of August 1944, with the front in Latvia being torn asunder by the Soviets, I Battalion was incorporated into the hastily formed Kampfgruppe "Wagner" of the III SS Panzer Corps (Germanic), and sent to a spot south of Tartu (Dorpat) to try and halt the communist advance into southern Estonia. The battalion entered the frontlines (facing south) next to the 11th East Prussian Infantry Division on 16 August.

On 19 August, I Battalion battled a strong enemy advance force at Patska and the nearby "Windmill" Hill. With the help of four German tanks, the Walloons were able to hold on to their lines, but elsewhere the Soviets made breakthroughs. By 21 August the battalion was defending the village of Kambi, and it threw back numerous attacks on the 21st and 22nd. On 23 August the Soviets took the town of Noo which not only threatened the Kambi positions, but the main road to Tartu as well. It so happened that the last defenders on the Tartu road turned out to be a small contingent of Walloon volunteers with three anti-tank guns led by Untersturmführer Leon Gillis.

The Soviets launched violent tank and infantry attacks against Gillis' positions, only to be thrown back again and again by the stubborn Walloons. Finally, after destroying all three anti-tank guns, the Reds seemed to have the situation in hand. Another assault force led by three T-34 tanks hurtled down the road. But Ustuf. Gillis rallied his men and led them, including the wounded, in a vigorous counterattack. Each of the tanks was knocked out by hand and the Soviets were routed. Gillis probably saved the Estonian Front that day. His achievement was recognized later with the award of the Knight's Cross.

On 24 August, I Battalion was ordered to hold on to the high ground near Kambi at all costs. But even with the help of the Stuka squadron led by Hans-Ulrich Rudel, this proved not to be possible. Two columns of Soviet tanks threatened the battalion with encirclement, and Stubaf. Degrelle was forced to lead his troops in a fighting retreat to the northwest. After establishing themselves just south of the Embach River, the Walloons counterattacked the enemy spearheads that night and achieved some local success.

The next day saw the battle for Tartu begin. It soon became apparent that the city couldn't be saved, but it was still possible to salvage the main defensive lines with a little effort. With that in mind, I Battalion held on to Boella, west of Tartu, in a day of intense fighting before relocating to the high ground to the north of Tartu. Here the battalion was deployed around Parma, Lombi and Keerov and again the orders were explicit: "The enemy must not get through." By using everyone he had, including drivers, clerical personnel and the lightly wounded, Stubaf. Degrelle was able to hold the front lines. But as night fell, the last "Wallonien" anti-tank gun was knocked out and Ustuf. Gillis was badly wounded.

For the next several days the Walloons maintained their positions, repulsing every communist attack. The battalion proved itself to be the most consistent and dependable unit along the entire front and won three favorable mentions in the III SS Panzer Corps war diary. But the Soviets had had enough; they wanted the tenacious Belgians out of the way—permanently. On 30 August, they launched mass attacks against the "Wallonien" positions every thirty minutes all day long. Despite this they still couldn't get through. The only way they could have succeeded was by killing every one of the Walloons and they came very close to doing just that. Of the 260 soldiers still with the battalion on the morning of 30 August, only thirty-two were still left alive and unwounded by evening.

The "Wallonien" contribution to the defensive victory north of Tartu was a substantial one, and every one of the battalion's survivors was decorated with the Iron Cross. Leon Degrelle received the Oakleaves to the Knight's Cross for his leadership. When the time came to transfer I Battalion back to Germany, Obergruppenführer Steiner, the commander of III SS Panzer Corps, held a last inspection of the battered unit and personally shook hands with each survivor. Finally he gave a short speech to them to thank them for their heroic accomplishments and he ended up by stating: "One Wallonien is worth a thousand ordinary soldiers." It would be hard to top that compliment.

The "Wallonien"

Chapter 5

Formation and Deployment of the 28th Volunteer Panzergrenadier Division "Wallonien"

The "Wallonien" Brigade began forming into the 28th SS Division on 20 September 1944, first in the Breslau area then later in South Hannover and Braunschweig. New recruits came from the large number of Belgian and French refugees who had flocked to Germany in the wake of the Allied invasion. A substantial number of Spaniards, from the thousand-man "Blue" Legion, also volunteered to serve with the "Wallonien" Division due in large measure to the personal appeal of its acting commander, Obersturmführer Leon Degrelle

In December 1944, a part of the 28th SS Division led by Ostubaf. (soon to be Standartenführer) Degrelle, was sent to the Ardennes sector that had been retaken by Sepp Dietrich's 6th Panzer Army. It was hoped to be able to send both the Flemish 27th and Walloon 28th SS Divisions back to Belgium when that country was recaptured. This of course did not come to pass, and in the latter part of January 1945, the ""Wallonien" Division was ordered to assemble all of its battle-worthy elements into a task force for use on the Eastern Front. The resulting battle-group contained the following units:

- Divisional staff
- SS Artillery Abteilung 28 (nucleus of the SS Artillery Regiment 28, but here just an artillery unit of unspecified size)
- SS Volunteer Panzergrenadier Regiment 69 under the command of Stubaf. Frans Hellebaut
- SS Volunteer Panzergrenadier Regiment 70 under the command of Stubaf. Jules Mathieu
- Total strength: around 4,000 men

According to Taylor, in *Uniforms, History and Organization of the Waffen-SS, Vol. 5*, a German officer, SS-Brigadeführer Nicholas Heilmann (formerly commanding officer of the 15th Latvian SS Division) had supplanted Leon Degrelle as commander of the "Wallonien." However, Heilmann was killed almost immediately after the 28th SS Division reached the Pomeranian sector and was replaced by Ostubaf. Degrelle

On 30 January 1945, Kampfgruppe "Wallonien" left the Niederaussem-Rheydt area for Stargard and Stettin. The rail journey took seven days, and after arriving at the Altdamm railroad station on 5 February, the Walloon units were quickly sent to defensive positions to the south and east of Stargard. In place next to KGr. "Wallonien" were two battalions from the 27th SS Division "Langemarck" (I Battalion, 66th Regiment and I Battalion, 67th Regiment), which arrived at the front on the same day as the "Wallonien."

The two Belgian SS divisional battle-groups were part of the III SS Panzer Corps, which held a long defensive sector facing south, stretching from Lake Madu in the west to Reetz and Nantikow in the east. All told, the Corps could only manage to deploy about fifteen thousand troops of virtually every West European nationality, while the opposing enemy forces of the 61st Soviet Red Army consisted of some ninety thousand men in nine full-strength divisions.

On 7 February, Soviet units had managed to take the key towns of Reetz and Hasendorf, which had been defended by troops from the 23rd Dutch SS Division "Nederland," and gained access to Reich Highway 104 which ran between Stettin and Reetz. On 8 February, the Soviets shifted their focus towards capturing the garrison town of Arnswalde, which meant that the Walloons would be directly involved in the fighting. The "Wallonien" units on this day were positioned as follows: I Battalion, 69 Regiment, around Repplin, II Battalion, 69th Regiment, between Kolin and Strebelow, I Battalion, 70th Regiment, between Schoeneberg and Arnswalde (about 4 km from Arnswalde). II Battalion, 70th Regiment, and the SS Artillery Abteilung 28 were being held in reserve.

The first "Wallonien" unit to be engaged on 8 February was the Battalion "Lakaie" or I Battalion, 70th Regiment, which was defending the Arnswalde turnoff on Highway 104. The enemy spearhead was stopped at Muscherin by the Company "Vermeiren" from I Battalion, 70th Regiment. There was also much violent fighting at Repplin where I Battalion, 69th Regiment, also managed to rebuff the Soviets. After the enemy movement had been halted in the "Wallonien" sector, the battle-group received orders from Corps' headquarters to launch a diversionary attack towards the south on the next day.

At daybreak on 9 February 1945, Ostubaf. Degrelle personally led the "Wallonien" attack. Advancing on both sides of Strebelow, the Walloons had a successful day, recapturing both Heinrichsthal and Karlsburg and taking control of the Linden Hills. A Soviet counterattack, with tanks, was driven back. But to the west, an attack by the 37th Panzer Corps at Warnitz/Damnitz, had failed, and most of the new "Wallonien" positions were jeopardized. Therefore a tactical withdrawal had to be carried out during the night to avoid encirclement. On 10 February, the enemy occupied Kruessow and a Wallonien volunteer company tried unsuccessfully to retake it. The "Wallonien" still maintained one company in the Linden Hills, but its position was very precarious.

The next big enemy threat came on 12 February, when the Soviets again tried to break through near Repplin but were thrown back in savage fighting by the Walloon Battalion "Derrickx" (I Battalion, 69th Regiment, commanded by Stubaf. Henri Derrickx).

The Arnswalde garrison, consisting of three thousand rocket-mortar training troops and some other Army elements, had been totally cut off, and III SS Panzer Corps was ordered to go to the rescue. The 10th SS Panzer Division "Frundsberg," the 11th SS Panzergrenadier Division "Nordland" and part of the 4th SS Polizei Panzergrenadier Division, were to spearhead the relief effort by attacking through the lines held by "Wallonien" and "Langemarck."

By the afternoon of 16 February, the III SS Panzer Corps divisions were advancing to the south in all sectors. "Frundsberg" managed to drive to the south point of Lake Madu where it was supposed to turn east and then link up with troops from the 4th SS Polizei Division to form a pocket around the Soviet forces between Lake Madu and Arnswalde. On 17 February, "Wallonien" was ordered to attack south through the Linden Hills between "Frundsberg" and the "Polizei" Division, but powerful enemy units went over on the counterattack and no "pocket" could be formed. Both "Frundsberg" and "Polizei" lost ground and the "Wallonien" assault never really got underway. In the Linden Hills, the Walloon volunteer company led by Ustuf. Capelle came under Soviet attack from three sides, but held onto its ground. Sixty-one wounded members of Capelle's company were evacuated and the remainder fought it out to the death in hand-to-hand combat against "Josef Stalin II" tanks. There were only four survivors of the final death struggle. But Capelle's men had bought III SS Panzer Corps twenty-four hours of precious time. Later on Ustuf. Capelle would be mentioned in the Wehrmacht War Communiqué and also be posthumously recommended for the Knight's Cross.

During the night of 17/18 February 1945 a relief corridor was constructed to Arnswalde and it proved possible to evacuate all of the trapped soldiers and civilians, thanks in no small measure to the sacrifices of the "Wallonien" Division. On 21 February, the "Wallonien," "Langemarck," "Nordland" and "Nederland" Divisions were pulled back over the Inha River to try and prepare for the expected enemy onslaught towards Stargard.

SS-Kampfgruppe "Wallonien" was repositioned along both sides of Kremzow on 22 February and maintained tenuous contact with the battalions of SS-Kampfgruppe "Langemarck," which were in place around Zadelow and Zachan. On 28 February the Soviets began probing attacks all along the III SS Panzer Corps front in preparation for their big drive towards Stettin. This began early on 1 March, following the greatest massed artillery barrage that the veteran troops from the III SS Corps had ever experienced. Many small defensive positions were simply wiped out altogether in the shell fire, making it all the more easy for the enemy to achieve significant penetrations.

Troops from the "Wallonien" Division held firm against the Soviet spearheads in Collin and Strebelow, so the enemy just began to bypass these towns with the objective of outflanking them. When ammunition began to run low, Standartenführer Degrelle ordered his battalions to fall back and regroup around Kremzow. Kremzow was the last strongpoint on the road to Stargard and the Walloons were just able to deploy there in time to stop the Soviets.

The next day, 2 March 1945, found the "Wallonien" holding on to its positions southeast of Stargard between Streesen and

Kremzow. Sturmbannführer Mathieu's SS Regiment 70 put up a particularly fierce resistance to the enemy on this day. But to the east of the Walloon SS troops the SS-Kampfgruppe "Langemarck" was forced to withdraw from the towns of Wulkow and Zartzig.

"Wallonien" had to begin a fighting withdrawal back towards Stargard on 3 March. The Belgians were able to repulse strong enemy vanguard elements at Kluetzow and Wittichow. Late in the day, elements of the "Wallonien" were shifted to defensive positions in the northern and western sections of Stargard. In the early hours of 4 March, Stargard had to be abandoned and the III SS Panzer Corps defenders were sent to a new line of villages between Stargard and Stettin. "Wallonien" battalions were dispatched to Luebow, Saarow and Seefeld, but their southern flank was left open when Soviet forces captured the north shore of Lake Madu. The situation could only be described as extremely dangerous.

March 5th proved to be a day of desperate fighting. SS-Kampfgruppe "Wallonien" held positions on both banks of the Inha River at Luebow and Saarow. The left, or east bank was composed of defensible high ground with many clumps of trees, but the right, or west bank consisted of flat empty land stretching away to the houses of Luebow. It was perfect tank country, as a strong force of fifteen Soviet tanks with accompanying infantry soon discovered. The Walloon battalion defending Luebow had run out of anti-tank weapons and couldn't stop the Red armor. After taking fifty per cent losses, the survivors of the battalion crossed the Inha under fire to Saarow.

The enemy assault on Saarow was more deliberate but just as deadly. Twenty-one heavy tanks rolled up towards the southern outskirts of the town, firing as they went. One building after another began to collapse under the impact of the tank shells, and the tanks gradually began moving into the town proper. One Walloon volunteer, who had been hiding behind a church door, suddenly jumped out and fired a Panzerfaust at the lead Soviet tank, setting it ablaze. This caused a panic in the enemy ranks and the attack abruptly halted, giving the Walloons enough breathing space to make a withdrawal to the west.

But at Seefeld, where the divisional headquarters and the artillery detachment were located, yet another severe crisis developed. No fewer than forty-one enemy tanks began to attack this village.

Standartenführer Degrelle personally directed his artillery batteries as they fired upon them at point-blank range. Finally the bravery and accuracy of the Walloon gunners turned the tide and the Soviets broke off their assault.

III SS Panzer Corps now had one last defensive bastion to man before retiring on the Oder River line; this was the Altdamm bridgehead near Stettin, and on 7 and 8 March 1945, most of the Corps' units were making their way back towards it. The perimeter of the bridgehead was defended by the "Nordland," "Frundsberg," "Nederland," "Langemarck" and "Wallonien" Divisions along with assorted Army, Navy and Air Force leftover infantry units. The two Belgian SS battle-groups found themselves placed in the villages of Hoeckendorf and Finkenwalde on the morning of 8 March. That same day the battle for the bridgehead began and for the next several days the perimeter began to perceptibly shrink as the outnumbered Waffen-SS troops were pushed back step-by-step to the Oder River.

After a dozen days of vicious combat the decision was made to begin evacuating the Altdamm bridgehead. A special Walloon assault battalion of about five hundred men was formed, in Finkenwalde, drawing personnel from all the remaining "Wallonien" units. Its commander was Stubaf. Henri Derrickx (known as "Der Boss" to his men), and the battalion's mission was to hold the approaches to the Altdamm-Stettin railroad bridge at all costs. With the support of two German tanks, Derrickx and his command did just that, even wiping out a Soviet penetration along the Altdamm-Zollhaus road in the process.

The final III SS Panzer Corps withdrawal from Altdamm to Stettin on the west bank of the Oder took place during the night of 19 March. The Autobahn bridge was defended until midnight by the machine-pistol platoon of SS Panzergrenadier Regiment 24 "Danmark" from the "Nordland" Division. After this unit crossed over, it was blown up. Fifteen hundred meters to the south, the SS Battalion "Derrickx" successfully kept open the railroad bridge until the early morning hours of 20 March before it, too, was destroyed after the Walloons and their tank escort had passed over. For his leadership during this difficult period of time, Stubaf. Henri Derrickx was awarded the German Cross in Gold. With the destruction of the last Oder bridges, the battle for Pomerania was

　　　　　　　　　　　　　　The "Wallonien"

finished but the struggle for the heart of the German Reich had just begun.

The "Wallonien"

Chapter 6

Last Battles of
the "Wallonien" Division

A fter all of the territory east of the Oder River had been evacuated by the Germans, there was a short hiatus in the main fighting while the Soviets rebuilt their strength and completed their reign of terror in the newly-occupied German territories. The Germans also tried to use this breathing spell to refurbish their forces, but by this stage of the war this was a nearly impossible task. Nonetheless, the 28th SS Division "Wallonien" began to reform in the towns of Schmagerow, Loecknitz and Bergholz, using troops that had been in training around Hannover, recovered wounded and new recruits. Amazing as it may sound there were still new Belgian recruits at this late stage of events. Fully one hundred Walloon volunteers who had been working in German factories turned up at the divisional headquarters, were issued field-gray SS uniforms, and began their training in very close proximity to the front.

On paper, the "Wallonien" Division was supposed to look like this:

- Staff
- SS Volunteer Panzergrenadier Regiment 69
- SS Volunteer Panzergrenadier Regiment 70
- SS Volunteer Panzergrenadier Regiment 71
- SS Artillery Regiment 28
- SS Anti-tank Detachment 28 (assault guns)
- SS Engineer Battalion 28
- SS Flak Detachment 28
- SS Signals Battalion 28

But in reality, things were far different. Standartenführer Degrelle was forced to reorganize his unit into two regiments: a frontline regiment containing the best veterans of the "Wallonien" under the command of Stubaf. Hellebaut and one reserve regiment, which held the new recruits, recovered wounded, amputees and assorted odds and ends. This was just a temporary solution and it did not last long in practice under actual battlefield conditions. In his memoirs, Degrelle mentions that parts of a German infantry regiment and an artillery regiment were also subordinated to his command at this time.

In the middle of April 1945, Degrelle split his frontline regiment into two battalions of between 600 to 650 men each. He personally retained command of one battalion that was positioned about six kilometers to the west of the Autobahn bridge at Stettin, while the second battalion, led by Stubaf. Derrickx, was placed around Hohenzahden to the southwest of Stettin where it maintained a front of between two and four kilometers in length. In between the two "Wallonien" battalions was a weak battle-group from the 4th SS Polizei Division, which had the responsibility of containing the Soviet bridgehead that was in place around the city of Stettin.

On the morning of 20 April, the Soviets launched an assault on the "Polizei" Division troops opposite their bridgehead, and in a very short time an emergency situation had developed. The Walloon Battalion "Derrickx" was made a part of a larger task force under the command of Stubaf. Hellebaut. This Kampfgruppe contained the following elements:

- SS Battalion "Derrickx" (about 600 men)
- SS Battalion "Demulder" (originally II Battalion, Regiment 68, from the "Langemarck" Division, but numbers changed frequently as units were combined together and mixed up at this juncture; contained around 400 men)
- Seven assault guns and a company or so of escorting infantry from the Army Anti-tank Detachment "Kolberg" (125 men)

At 1400 hours on 20 April, SS-Kampfgruppe "Hellebaut" launched a counterattack along the Pommellen-Neu Rosow road in the direction of the southern portion of the Soviet bridgehead. Battalion "Demulder" hit the enemy at Kolbitzow, but could not hold its ground and was pushed back by vastly superior Soviet forces. All afternoon, Battalion "Derrickx" fought around Neu - Rossow with little to show for it. Late in the day, Stubaf. Derrickx took personal command of his 3rd Company and tried to push the enemy back across the river at Schillersdorf with it, but to no avail. The town remained firmly in enemy hands.

The sacrificial fighting began anew on 21 April, when Battalion "Demulder" was ordered to retake Schillersdorf. With the aid of fire support from an 88mm Flak gun battery, the brave Flemings attacked the Soviet positions again and again but could not gain headway. Finally Stubaf. Demulder was killed and most of the battalion's other officers were incapacitated. That virtually brought the unit's offensive efforts to an end.

The remainder of SS-Kampfgruppe "Hellebaut" was committed to action to the south of the Stettin Autobahn and was able to retake the town of Schoeningen. But at 1400 hours the attack had to be called off. There just weren't enough soldiers left and the Soviets were too powerful. Sturmbannführer Derrickx's battalion had taken 470 casualties and now totaled a mere 130 men. Obersturmbannführer Leon Gillis' 3rd Company, SS Anti-tank Detachment 28, which had been attached to Kampfgruppe "Hellebaut," had been reduced from 150 men to forty.

Things were not going too well either with Staf. Degrelle's Walloon battalion to the west of Stettin. On 21 April it carried out six separate counterattacks on the Soviet advance forces and by day's end there were only thirty-five men left out of the original 650. No one could ask for a better example of discipline and sacrifice. The next few days were marked by a steady—and sometimes chaotic—German withdrawal from the Oder Front. The 28th SS Division "Wallonien" came under the operational control of Divisional Group "Mueller," which also included the bulk of the 27th SS Division "Langemarck." This force was under the overall command of Oberführer Thomas Mueller, who was also the "Langemarck" commanding officer.

From 23 to 25 April, Divisional Group "Mueller" fell back towards the "Wotan Positions" along the Randow River to the north of Berlin. This was the last defensive line of any consequence on the northern part of the Eastern Front. On 25 April, part of "Wallonien" tried to eliminate a small Soviet bridgehead (only two companies' worth of defenders) across the Randow River near Bagemuehl, but even this task now proved to be too difficult. By the morning of 26 April, the enemy was breaking through at will along the Randow and the "Wotan Positions" were lost before they could even be fully occupied.

Falling back on his reserve regiment, Staf. Degrelle had been able to again put together two competent frontline battalions of perhaps five hundred men each. On 26 April they enjoyed some small success by blunting a Soviet drive at Menkin to the southeast of Pasewalk, but time was now clearly running out and everyone knew it. The next retreat took the Divisional Group "Mueller" to Prenzlau, one step ahead of the oncoming foe. The Uecker River and Uecker Lakes near here offered the last remote hope of even forming some sort of defensive positions, and one final effort was made to string up a line of resistance. On 27 April, the gallant "Hitler Youth" Battalion from the "Langemarck" Division (originally I Battalion, 68th Regiment) made a determined stand along the strand between the twin Uecker Lakes, but elsewhere it was the same old story; Prenzlau had to be abandoned late in the day after stiff fighting.

Late on 27 April, the "Wallonien" Division continued its retreat to the west, moving from Woldeck to the Neubrandenburg area. At Neubrandenburg an eight hundred man contingent from the 33rd SS Division "Charlemagne" (France No. 1), latched onto Divisional Group "Mueller,'" and joined the two Belgian SS divisions on their trek to the Allied lines in the west. On 30 April, the commanders of "Charlemagne," "Langemarck" and "Wallonien" held their first and only joint command conference in the small village of Nossentiner Huette. The "Langemarck" and "Charlemagne" commanders reluctantly decided that the time had come to allow their soldiers to surrender to the Western Allies. But Leon Degrelle of the "Wallonien" wanted to carry on the fight with his 800-man, two-battalion "division." He really had no choice personally, since he had been condemned to death *in absentia* by the reinstalled civilian government in Belgium and beyond that he held a fierce loyalty to his belief in the righteousness of the struggle against "international Bolshevism."

The odyssey of the "Wallonien" Division ended in the first week of May 1945 at Luebeck, Flensburg, and in Denmark where the last remnants of this fully tried and tested volunteer unit were forced to capitulate. But not Leon Degrelle. He first went to Norway where 300,000 undefeated German soldiers were still under arms, and when the surrender took effect there, he flew on to exile in Spain. He just barely made it over the frontier, before his aircraft (originally provided to Vidkun Quisling) crash-landed on a Spanish beach. But Degrelle survived to record the story of his Walloon volunteers in his epic work, *The Russian Campaign* (also published under two other titles).

The 28th SS Division "Wallonien" had done all that was required of it. Its soldiers had fought with skill, courage and idealism against a barbaric enemy, the Soviet Union that enslaved half of Europe under the pretext of liberating it. In the final accounting, four thousand Walloon volunteers fell on the Eastern Front; the ultimate testimony as to the courage and sacrifice of the "Wallonien" Legion, Brigade and Division.

- **Commander:** SS-Standartenführer Leon Degrelle
- **Operations Officer (Ia):** SS-Sturmbannführer Frans Hellebaut
- **Commander SS-Frw.Grn.Rgt. 69:** SS-Hauptsturmführer Jules Mathieu
- **Commander I./SS-Rgt. 69:** SS-Hauptsturmführer Henri Derrickx
- **Commander II./SS-Rgt. 69:** SS-Hauptsturmführer H. Lakaie
- **Commander 8./SS-Rgt. 69 (Heavy Weapons Company):** SS-Untersturmführer Charles Monfils
- **Commander 9./SS-Rgt. 69 (Anti-tank Company):** SS-Untersturmführer Guy Dupire
- **Commander SS-Frw.Grn.Rgt. 70:** SS-Sturmbannführer Georges Tchekhoff
- **Commander I./SS-Rgt. 70:** SS-Hauptsturmführer Georges Ruelle
- **Commander II./SS-Rgt. 70:** unknown
- **Commander SS-Frw.Grn.Rgt. 70:** unknown.
- **Commander SS-Artillerie Rgt. 28:** SS-Hauptsturmführer J. Malherbe
- **Commander SS-Panzerjäger Abt. 28 (Anti-tank and Flak Companies):** unknown.
- **Commander I./SS-Pz.Jg.Abt. 28:** SS-Obersturmführer Leon Gillis
- **Commander SS-Pioneer Btl. 28:** SS-Obersturmführer Joseph Mirgain
- **Commander SS-Nachrichten Abt. 28 (Signals):** SS-Obersturmführer Roger Wastiau
- **Commander SS-A.u.E. Btl. 36:** SS-Hauptsturmführer Dengis

Chapter 7

Europe in Cherkassy

Standartenführer Leon Degrelle (Commander of the 28th SS Division "Wallonien" and bearer of the Knight's Cross with Oakleaves), on the 30th Anniversary of the Cherkassy Pocket Breakout:

It is now thirty years since we fought side by side in Cherkassy; German comrades, comrades from Holland, Flanders, Denmark, Norway, the Baltic and we, the French-speaking Germanic Wallonien comrades. We gave our blood—thousands among us gave their lives—in the service of a great cause. In this bloody battle we fought for the true Europe, the Europe of two thousand years of culture. On the snowfields of Cherkassy we defended a great past and the construction of the future.

Our sacrifices and our dead have not immediately brought about victory. But I believe that our Europe was the TRUE Europe, it was not the Europe of the pitiful manipulators who put material interests above the public good; nor that of the clique of egotistical, petty politicians and their miserable avaricious [associates].

Our Europe was the Europe of high ideals and beliefs, held as a common bond. People did not die for a useless cause; they gave their youth and their lives to bring about a work of good. Our Europe was a Europe led by a strong hand, a Europe all-encompassing and large, from the end of the steppes to the Atlantic, supported by an immense healthy force, the force of the Waffen-SS; youth from twenty-eight European countries, one and another welded together, in the strength of a million, disciplined and with purpose, determined to accomplish their common goals.

This Europe had a soul, a meaning, it possessed then the only real, effective unity: that which is derived from devout faith. This was supported emphatically by the reality of our arms, our "troop," our ideals and our iron will, giving us the sure ability to endure any difficulties.

Sooner or later, this strong, idealistic Europe, as opposed to the Europe of the small-time politicians and manipulators, will become a reality. We believe this day will be coming soon comrades, and we have proven by our actions at Cherkassy and in the whole period of the great struggles of the Eastern Front, that some of the credit belongs to us.

Chapter 8

Portrait of a "Wallonien" Volunteer

SS-Sturmbannführer Henri Derrickx

Henri Derrickx was born in Belgium in 1904 of Flemish, Walloon, Dutch and German ancestry. His father was killed in the first days of World War I while serving with the Belgian Army. After completing his schooling, Derrickx began an active business career and eventually ended up representing the Petrofina finance group as a "diplomat-merchant" in the Belgian African colonies. He was also a reserve officer in the Belgian Army. Because of events in Europe, Derrickx was called back to Belgium in 1939 and found himself called to active Army duty with the rank of First Lieutenant.

In 1942, Derrickx volunteered for service with the Legion "Wallonie" which was fighting as a Wehrmacht mountain battalion on the Eastern Front. He entered the Legion with his old Belgian Army rank restored, and he was placed in charge of a platoon. A short time later he rose to the command of 2nd Company, which he led with great skill and proficiency. While at this position he received the nickname "Der Boss" from his men, and this would stick with him until his death.

When the Legion "Wallonie" was expanded into the 5th SS Sturmbrigade "Wallonien" in 1943, Derrickx remained a company commanding officer but received a promotion to the rank of Hauptsturmführer (Captain). Hauptsturmführer Derrickx was wounded in the battle for the Cherkassy-Korsun Envelopment, but despite this he remained at the head of his troops and succeeded in leading the last group of Walloon volunteers out of the entrapment.

In the summer of 1944, Henri Derrickx was promoted to Sturmbannführer (Major) and assigned the task of forming I Battalion, SS Panzergrenadier Regiment 69, for the new 28th SS Division "Wallonien." Derrickx became the personification of I Battalion, and through his fair-handed leadership, fully won the affection and loyalty of his soldiers. In 1945, Stubaf. Derrickx led I Battalion, 69th Regiment, in the hard battles along the Inha River, in Altdamm, Stettin and along the Oder. He commanded a reinforced battle-group that served very effectively as a rearguard for the last bridgehead on the east bank of the Oder River at Altdamm, and for his performance in this capacity, he received the coveted German Cross in Gold (one notch in prestige below the Knight's Cross). Among Derrickx's other decorations in the course of the war were both classes of the Iron Cross, and a grade of the Close Combat Clasp.

On 3 May 1945, Stubaf. Derrickx and the survivors of I Battalion, 69th Regiment, "Wallonien," entered American captivity in northern Germany. He was promptly returned to Belgium, where as a reward for his three hard years of fighting communism on the Eastern Front, he received a five year prison sentence. After his release from prison in 1950, Derrickx carved out a new business career for himself and married the widow of one of his former platoon leaders who had been killed in Russia. A superb soldier and fine example of a European Waffen-SS officer, Henri Derrickx died on 6 November 1972.

Chapter 9

Cherkassy Breakout Figures

- **Total strength of the two Army Corps prior to the breakout:** 49,000 (approximate)
- **Wounded airlifted out prior to the breakout:** 4,161
- **Actual number of troops to successfully break out:** 35,199
- **Unwounded:** 27,703
- **Wounded:** 7.4%
- **Wounded left behind:** at least 600 non-transportable
- **Killed or missing during the breakout:** 9,640—possibly up to 10,000

Unwounded "breakout" soldiers on duty as of 29 February 1944:

- **XXXXII Army Corps troops:** 606
- **XI Army Corps troops:** 848
- **88th Infantry Division:** 3,163
- **389th Infantry Division:** 1,889
- **72nd Infantry Division:** 3,615
- **57th Infantry Division:** 2,697
- **Corps Detachment B:** 4,831
- **5th SS "Wiking" (and "Wallonien"):** 8,253
- **Part of 213th Security Division:** 440
- **Part of 14th Panzer Division:** 465
- **Part of 168th Infantry Division:** 613
- **Assault Gun Brigade 239:** 150
- **1st Artillery Observer's Detachment:** 123
- **Total:** 27,703

Note: Figure for wounded left behind is included in the killed or missing since their fate is still not known.

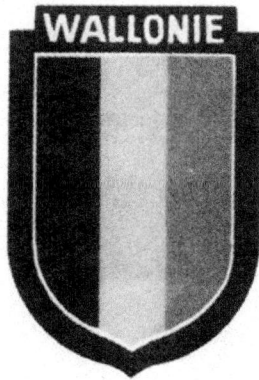

The "Wallonien"

Bibliography

Degrelle Leon. *Die Verlorene Legion*. West Germany: K.W. Schuetz Verlag, new edition, 1972.

Landwehr, Richard. "The European Volunteer Movement in World War II," *The Journal of Historical Review*, Vol. 2, No. 1, Spring 1981, pages 59-84.

—. *Narva 1944: The Waffen-SS and the Battle for Europe*. Silver Spring, Maryland: Bibliophile Legion Books, 1981.

—. *Lions of Flanders: Flemish Volunteers of the Waffen-SS, 1941-45*. Silver Spring, Maryland: Bibliophile Legion Books, 1983.

Littlejohn, David. *Foreign Legions of the Third Reich, Vol. 2*. San Jose, California: R. James Bender Publishing, 1982.

Roba, J. L. "The First Months of the Sturmbrigade "Wallonien," *Siegrunen*, Vol. 2 No. 2 (May 1978), and Vol. 2 No. 3 (July 1978).

Tieke, Wilhelm. *Tragodie urn die Treue*. West Germany: Munin-Verlag, third printing, 1978.

The "Wallonien"

Degrelle speaks as the leader of the Rexist Party. Notice the symbol of the party with a crown and a cross (Royalist and Catholic). [via J. L. Roba]

Symbol of the Rexist Party.

The "Wallonien"

Leon Degrelle as the leader of the Rex Party.

Degrelle is photographed with men of the collaboration police (Gardes Wallones). He wears the Army uniform in this photo taken before 1943. [via J. L. Roba]

The "Wallonien"

Degrelle as a private in the Legion "Wallonie."

Recruiting postcard.

The "Wallonien"

Recruiting postcard.

Color guard of the Legion "Wallonie."

The "Wallonien"

"Wallonien" battle pennant as shown on a recruiting postcard.

"Wallonie" Waffen-SS armshield.

"Wallonien" armband.

Proposed "Wallonien" collar patch.

Insignia of the 28th SS-Frw.-Pz.Gren.-Div. "Wallonie."

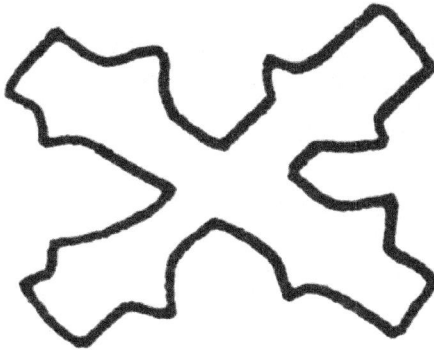

Insignia of the 28th SS-Frw.-Pz.Gren.-Div. "Wallonie."

Group of Walloon volunteers from Legion "Wallonie" just before being transferred into the Waffen-SS.

The "Wallonien"

Reichsführer-SS Himmler visits the "Wallonien" Brigade soon after it became a part of the Waffen-SS in the summer of 1943. Next to him, fourth from right, is Lucien Lippert, the Brigade commanding officer, still in Army uniform.

Degrelle and RF-SS Himmler at the creation of the Sturmbrigade.

The "Wallonien"

Degrelle firing a submachine gun on the Eastern Front. Hitler said to him: "You are almost unique in history, a political leader who fights as a true soldier."

Leon Degrelle, Legion "Wallonie," 1942.

The "Wallonien"

Volunteers for the 5th SS Sturmbrigade "Wallonien" line up behind the company colors.

"Wallonien" field mass.

The "Wallonien"

SS-Stubaf. Degrelle and other "Wallonien" officers.

Soldiers of the "Wallonien" with a Flak gun which was used against ground troops and other targets in the terrible fighting around Korsun. [Centre d'Etudes de la seconde Guerre Mondiale, Brussels, via J. L. Roba]

The "Wallonien"

An exhausted Waffen-SS soldier in a Russian village. Note the German material in the background. [Centre d'Etudes de la seconde Guerre Mondiale, Brussels, via J. L. Roba]

The "Wallonien"

Walloon volunteers from the Sturmbrigade at about the time of the Cher-kassy fighting.

The "Wallonien"

"Walloon" SS volunteers near Cherkassy.

Estonian member of the SS-Battalion "Narwa" with the "Wiking" Division at Cherkassy loading shell number 4,000 in his "Wespe" self-propelled gun. [via Kenneth Nieman]

The "Wallonien"

Goroditsche-Korsun road on 8 February 1944.

16 February 1944: Last preparations for the breakout at Schanderovka.

The "Wallonien"

Waffen-SS troops during the Cherkassy breakout.

Waffen-SS troops during the Cherkassy breakout.

The "Wallonien"

Heroes of Cherkassy receiving decorations.

Orchids for the heroes of Cherkassy, Brussels, April 1944.

The "Wallonien"

Degrelle receiving the Knight's Cross from Hitler after Cherkassy, February 1944. In the center is SS-Gruf. Gille, commanding officer of the "Wiking" Division. Next to him is SS-Brigfhr. Fegelein, Waffen-SS liaison officer to the Führer's headquarters.

Estonia, August 1944. Degrelle as commanding officer of SS-Kampfgruppe "Wallonien" along with SS-Brigadeführer Jürgen Wagner, left, commander of 4.SS-Pz.Gr.Bde. "Nederland" and SS-KGr. "Wagner." On the right is the "Nederland" brigade adjutant, SS-Ostuf. Schaefer.

Degrelle receives Oakleaves from Hitler, August 1944.

SS-Hstuf. Leon Degrelle.

The "Wallonien"

Belgian Rex-Bewegnung Award. This medal was given to members of the "Wallonien" Division. It depicts a vertical sword over a pair of crossed rose stems surrounded by the words "BRAVOURE — HONNEUR — FEDELITE" (Bravery — Honor — Fidelity).

The photos show a Walloon officer and two NCOs with the Belgian Rex-Bewegnung Award on their breast pocket.

The "Wallonien"

The "Wallonien"

Belgian volunteer from the 28th SS Division "Wallonien." Note the Rex-Bewegnung Award on his breast pocket.

The "Wallonien"

Men of the Sturmbrigade "Wallonien" running a phone line in 1943. The car is a Horch. [Centre d'Etudes de la seconde Guerre Mondiale, Brussels, via J. L. Roba]

Signalmen of the "Wallonien." Note the insignia on the left arm: the national shield with the three colors (black, yellow, red) and the title "Wallonie"; also, the "blitz" (lightning) insignia for the signal personnel of non-signal units. [Centre d'Etudes de la seconde Guerre Mondiale, Brussels, via J. L. Roba]

The "Wallonien"

The personalities at the front of the town hall: On the first step, left to right—Witt, Raeder and his 'aide de camp'; second step—Wuensche (in his black uniform and his Ritterkreuz) and Degrelle; third step—Meyer and Mohnke. All others are men of the SS or the Wehrmacht. [via J. L. Roba]

Some more personalities at the front of the town hall: Men of the collaboration police and a few soldiers of lower rank. Notice the Untersturmführer with his Belgian shield. [via J. L. Roba]

The "Wallonien"

Degrelle in his car at the "Place du Manege." [via J. L. Roba]

A Sd.Kfz. 251 carries one of the flags of the Sturmbrigade. [via J. L. Roba]

The "Wallonien"

Entry of the vehicles in Charleroi. A Sd.Kfz. 7/2 (late model) with a 37mm Flak gun is certainly one of those lent to the "Wallonien" by the "Hitler Jugend." [via J. L. Roba]

The entry into Brussels. A "Stummel" (Sd.Kfz. 251/9) loaded with men of the "Wallonien" is greeted by the crowd. [Centre d'Etudes de la seconde Guerre Mondiale, Brussels, via J. L. Roba]

Degrelle and his children in the Sd.Kfz. 251 half-track at the homecoming in Brussels.

Degrelle and his children in the Sd.Kfz. 251 half-track at the homecoming in Brussels.

The "Wallonien"

Degrelle in his Sd.Kfz. 251 half-track salutes his men at the front of the "Bourse." [Centre d'Etudes de la seconde Guerre Mondiale, Brussels, via J. L. Roba]

The children of the Rexist leader with their father in his Sd.Kfz. 251 half-track. [Centre d'Etudes de la seconde Guerre Mondiale, Brussels, via J. L. Roba]

The "Wallonien"

Degrelle as commander of the "Wallonien" Division in 1945.

Semi-postal stamps issued for the Legion "Wallonie." Semi-postals were issued to financially aid the organization depicted on the stamps. Besides the amount paid for use of the stamp to pay for normal postage, an additional amount was paid which was turned over to the organization.

TIMBRES DE FRANCHISE

DE LA LEGION DES VOLONTAIRES
WALLONS CONTRE LE BOLCHEVISME

TIMBRES DE FRANCHISE

DE LA LEGION DES VOLONTAIRES
WALLONS CONTRE LE BOLCHEVISME

The "Wallonien"

Leon Degreelle stamp.

Cover of booklet of ten Leon Degrelle stamps.

Walloon and Flemish Waffen-SS volunteers marching through Antwerp with their respective flags.

The "Wallonien"

Leon Gillis, "Wallonien" Knight's Cross winner under Degrelle.

Ostubaf. Lucien Lippert, 1st Brigade commanding officer.

The "Wallonien"

Ostuf. Hans Drexel, operations officer for the Sturmbrigade (German).

Waffen-SS officer candidates from twelve different countries.

The "Wallonien"

Young soldiers of the "Wallonien" Division at Stettin, 1945. Second from left: SS-Ustuf. Jacques Leroy, the third Walloon to be awarded the Knight's Cross. Center: SS-Ustuf. Andre Regibeau, commanding officer of the 1st Company, SS-Regiment 69. Right: The French SS volunteer Thuilliez.

Memorial service on the 30th anniversary of the Cherkassy Breakout. Danish, German, Flemish and Walloon veterans of the battle are shown.

Leon Degrelle in 1975.

The "Wallonien"

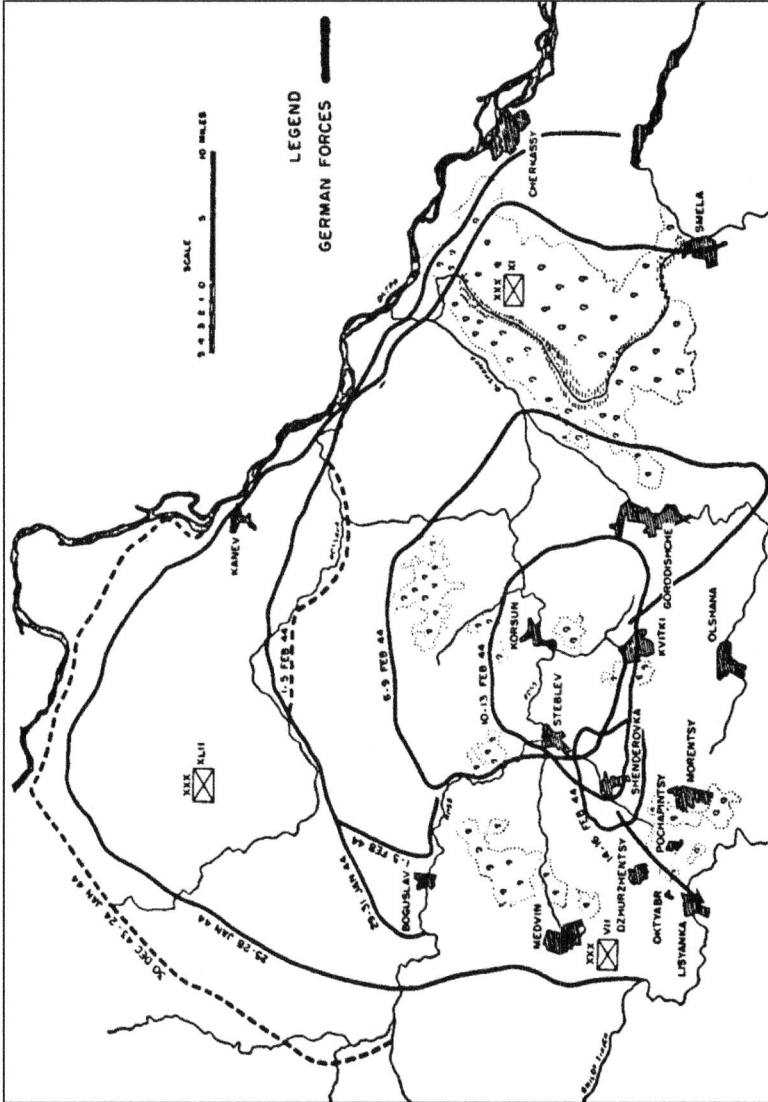

The Pocket West of Cherkassy

Breakout to Lisyanka — Situation 16 and 17 February 1944

The "Wallonien"

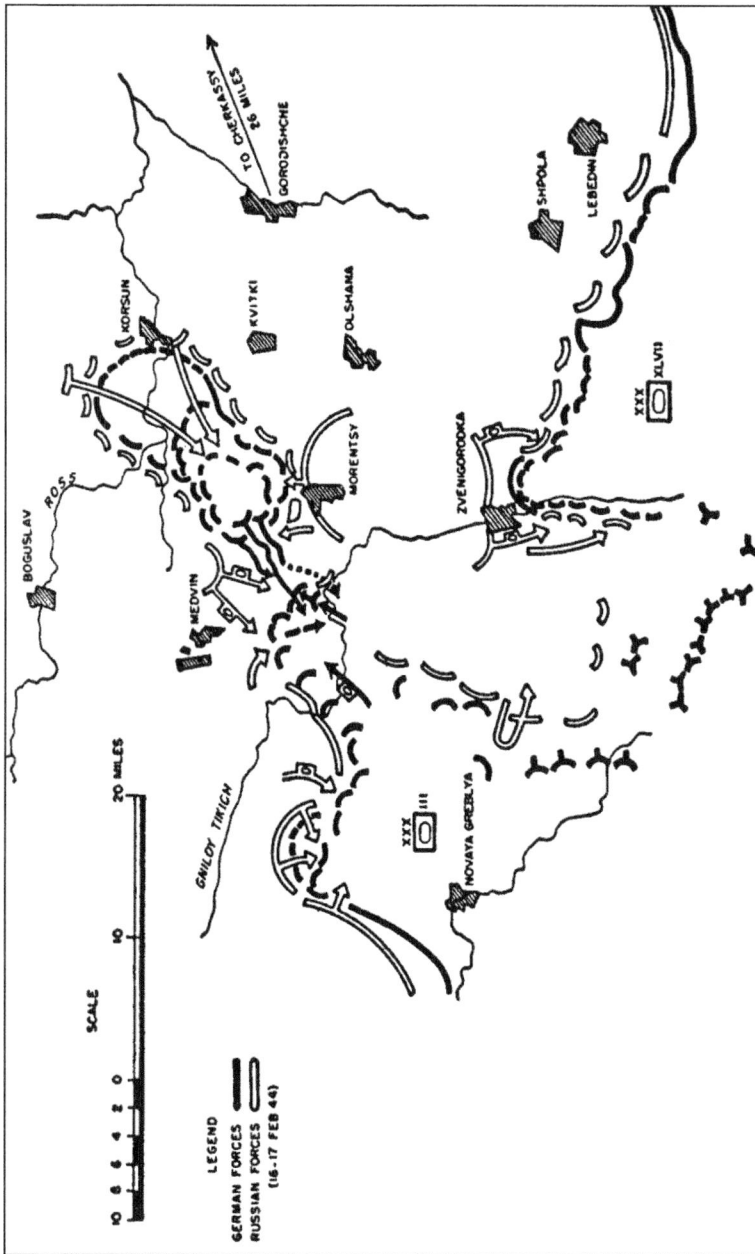

Relief Attempts.

Offensive Operations of the III SS Panzer Corps in the Arnswalde sector, 16-18 February 1945.

120   The "Wallonien"

Walloon Legion

The Walloon Legion (French: Légion Wallonie) was a collaborationist military formation recruited among French-speaking volunteers from German-occupied Belgium, notably from Brussels and Wallonia, during World War II. It was formed in the aftermath of the German invasion of the Soviet Union and fought on the Eastern Front as part of the German Army (Wehrmacht) and later the Waffen SS alongside similar formations from other parts of German-occupied Europe.

Established in July 1941, the Walloon Legion was envisaged by Léon Degrelle's Rexist Party as a means of demonstrating its loyalty and political indispensability in German-occupied Belgium where it had been largely ignored since the German invasion of May 1940. A similar formation had already been created by Flemish collaborators as the Flemish Legion, preventing Degrelle from being able to establish the "Belgian Legion" he had originally intended. The Walloon Legion, initially part of the Wehrmacht, remained no larger than a battalion and was joined by Degrelle himself who increasingly saw the unit as a more important political vehicle than the Rexist Party. It participated in fighting on the Eastern Front from February 1942 but struggled to find sufficient recruits in Belgium to replace its persistently heavy losses.

The unit was integrated into the Waffen-SS in June 1943 as the SS-Sturmbrigade Wallonia and was almost destroyed by Soviet forces in the Korsun–Cherkassy Pocket in February 1944. It expanded slightly after the Allied Liberation of Belgium in September 1944 as Belgian, French, and Spanish collaborators were drafted in and was upgraded to the notional status of a division. After heavy losses and desertions, its remaining personnel surrendered to British forces in April 1945.

BACKGROUND

At the time of the German invasion in May 1940, Belgium had several political parties that were broadly sympathetic to the authoritarian and anti-democratic ideals represented by Nazi Germany. In Wallonia and Brussels, the largest of these groups was the Rexist Party, led by Léon Degrelle. This had originated as a faction of the mainstream Catholic Block, but split in 1935 to form an independent populist party. Ideologically, Rex supported Belgian nationalism, but its support for corporatism and anti-communism made it sympathetic towards aspects of Nazi ideology. It achieved some early success, peaking at the elections of 1936 in which it received 11.5 percent of the national vote. In spite of this, the party experienced a rapid decline in the years before the German invasion and polled below five percent in the 1939 elections and remained marginal.

After the Belgian surrender on 28 May 1940, a German Military Administration was created to govern the occupied territory. Preferring a strategy of indirect rule, the administration preferred to work with established Belgian political and social elites, largely ignoring fringe political groups such as the Rexists.

CREATION OF THE WALLOON LEGION, 1941–42

In order to acquire more influence and German support, Rex attempted to bring itself closer to the occupation authorities. On 1 January 1941, Degrelle announced Rex's total support for the occupation authorities and for the policy of collaborationism. After the German invasion of the Soviet Union on 22 June 1941, it embraced the idea of raising a military unit, seen as "a political opportunity to increase the importance of their movements and eliminate political competition". At the same time, the Flemish National Union (Vlaams Nationaal Verbond, VNV), a Flemish nationalist and rival authoritarian party in Flanders, also announced its intention to form a "Flemish Legion" to fight in the German Army in the Soviet Union. This move, combined with the Germans' favorable stance towards the VNV, meant that it would not be possible to realize Rex's preferred option of a national "Belgian Legion" on the Eastern Front.

In July 1941, Rex announced that it would raise a unit of volunteers of its own, dubbed the Walloon Legion (Légion Wallonie). Unlike comparable Flemish and Dutch units, the Walloon Legion was established within the German Army (Wehrmacht) because Walloons were not considered sufficiently "Germanic" by Nazi racial theorists be allowed into the Waffen-SS. Recruitment initially met with little success, leading Degrelle personally to volunteer for the unit as a private as a publicity stunt. In total, some 850 men had volunteered by August 1941, bringing the unit up to the strength of a battalion. Officially designated as Infantry Battalion 373 (Infanterie Bataillon 373), it was sent for training in Meseritz in Germany. As part of Degrelle's ideal of an expanded Burgundian-style Belgium, the unit adopted the Cross of Burgundy as its insignia.

Most of the Legion's initial volunteers were Rexist cadres and many had been part of the Combat Formations (Formations de Combat) which served as the party's paramilitary wing. In propaganda, Rex emphasized the anti-communist dimension of the German war effort and argued that collaboration was compatible with Belgian patriotism. The unit encountered various internal problems with some volunteers being unwilling to swear personal allegiance to Adolf Hitler and others being classed as medically unfit; almost a third of the volunteers were repatriated before October 1941. Over the winter of 1941–1942, it participated in training and anti-partisan operations near Donetsk in the Ukraine.

EASTERN FRONT

In the Wehrmacht, 1942–43

The Walloon Legion fought its first engagement against Soviet forces at Gromowaja-Balka, near Donetsk, on 28 February 1942 as part of the 17th Army. It suffered heavy losses, both from disease and combat, and was reduced to 150 men within its first months. It continued to encounter "enormous losses" throughout 1942. Its record in combat, however, was widely exploited in propaganda and increased Degrelle's legitimacy in the eyes of the German leadership, especially Heinrich Himmler who commanded the SS. In late 1942, Himmler declared the Walloons to be a Germanic race, paving the way for the unit's incorporation into the Waffen-SS on 1 June 1943. The Walloon Legion was re-organised into an brigade-sized unit of 2,000 men, known as the SS-Sturmbrigade Wallonia (SS- Sturmbrigade Wallonien).

The high attrition rate within the Walloon Legion required increasing focus on recruitment. A second recruitment drive was started in February 1942, recruiting 450 new volunteers of whom many came from Rex's small youth wing. A third "frantic" campaign in November 1942 raised a further 1,700 men. These recruitment drives weakened many Rexist institutions by diverting manpower away from projects in Belgium. At the same time, it failed to secure significant numbers of recruits from among the Belgian prisoners of war held in German camps. However, Degrelle became increasingly keen on the political potential of the Walloon Legion which he saw as a more effective political tool than the Rexist Party in Belgium. As the war continued and the pool of Rexist members fell, the volunteers became "largely non-political 'adventurers' or desperate men", often drawn from the urban working class and the unemployed.

In the Waffen-SS, 1943–45

In November 1943, the new SS-Sturmbrigade Wallonia was deployed for the first time to the Ukraine in response to the Soviet Dnieper–Carpathian Offensive. There, the brigade fought as part of the SS Wiking Panzer Division in the Korsun–Cherkassy Pocket in February 1944 and suffered 70 percent casualties. Among those killed was the unit's commander Lucien Lippert. A detachment also fought at the Tannenberg Line in Estonia in June 1944, also suffering heavy losses. Degrelle, however, was widely celebrated for his role in the battle at Cherkassy and received the Knight's Cross, becoming "the poster boy for all European collaborators" and being featured in Signal magazine. The remnants of the unit returned to Belgium where parades were held in Brussels and Charleroi in April 1944. Ahead of its return, largely to encourage more enlistments, the unit was even loaned armored vehicles by other German units to make it seem more prestigious.

In the aftermath of the Allied Liberation of Belgium in September 1944, Degrelle managed to get the brigade upgraded to division-status, after drafting Rexist refugees fleeing the Allied advance and Walloon volunteers from the paramilitary National Socialist Motor Corps (NSKK). The new 28th SS Volunteer Grenadier Division "Wallonia" (28. SS-Freiwilligen-Grenadier-Division Wallonien) was created in October 1944. It numbered fewer than 4,000 men, making it considerably understrength, and French and Spanish soldiers from the Legion of French Volunteers Against

Bolshevism (LVF) and Blue Legion were folded into the unit to increase its numbers. During the retreat, Walloon soldiers participated in the massacre of 6,000 Jewish female prisoners of Stutthof concentration camp in January 1945. The following month, the remains of the "division" saw action during Operation Solstice and were forced to retreat through Central Pomerania to Stettin on the Oder river. After mass defections in April its remaining 400 personnel fled to Lübeck in Schleswig-Holstein where they surrendered to the British Army to escape capture by Soviet forces.

Altogether, between 7,000 and 8,000 men served in the Walloon Legion between 1941 and 1944, slightly less than the number of Flemish who served in comparable formations. Some 1,337 were killed, representing about a fifth of its total strength. However, its maximum field strength had never exceeded 2,000 men. Fearing execution for treason in Belgium, Degrelle escaped to Denmark and Norway and then fled to Francoist Spain where he remained in exile until his death in 1994.

BIBLIOGRAPHY

- Plisnier, Flore (2011). Ils ont pris les armes pour Hitler: la collaboration armée en Belgique francophone. Brussels: Renaissance du Livre.
- Wouters, Nico (2018). "Belgium". In Stahel, David (ed.). Joining Hitler's Crusade: European Nations and the Invasion of the Soviet Union, 1941. Cambridge: Cambridge University Press. pp. 260–287.
- Aron, Paul; Gotovitch, José, eds. (2008). "Légion Wallonie". Dictionnaire de la seconde guerre mondiale en Belgique. Brussels: André Versaille. pp. 243–245.

Further Reading

- Conway, Martin (1993). Collaboration in Belgium: Léon Degrelle and the Rexist Movement, 1940-1944. New Haven: Yale University Press.
- De Bruyne, Eddy (1991). Les Wallons meurent à l'est: la Légion Wallonie et Léon Degrelle sur le Front russe, 1941-1945. Paris: Didier Hatier.

- Littlejohn, David (1972). The Patriotic Traitors: A History of Collaboration in German-occupied Europe, 1940-45. London: Heinemann.

Insignia of the Walloon Legion, incorporating the flag of Belgium rather than any distinctly "Walloon" symbolism.

The "Wallonien"

Recruitment poster for the Walloon Legion, appealing to Belgian nationalist and anti-communist sentiment. The caption reads "You defend Belgium... by fighting on the Eastern Front". 1943.

Léon Degrelle, leader of Rex and member of the Walloon Legion, pictured in Charleroi in April 1944. Degrelle saw the Legion as a political tool to gain German support.

The "Wallonien"

The "Wallonien"

The banner reads: V Allemagne victorieuse sur tout le front

The "Wallonien"

The "Wallonien"

The "Wallonien"

Leon Degrelle in Spain, 1949.

The "Wallonien"

The "Wallonien"

The "Wallonien"

Noncommissioned officers of the "Wallonien" at officer training in Bad Tölz, Germany.

Walloon volunteers in the Cherkassy Pocket, December 1943.

The "Wallonien"

Pomerania, February-March, 1945. From left to right: Ustuf Georges Suain, Ustuf Leon Gillis, Ustuf Desire Lecocq, Oscha Van Isschott, and Sturmmann Collard.

The "Wallonien"

Leon Degrelle, a highly decorated combat veteran, talks with factory workers in his native country.

Leon Degrelle, second from right.

The "Wallonien"

The "Wallonien"

Recruiting postcard.

The "Wallonien"

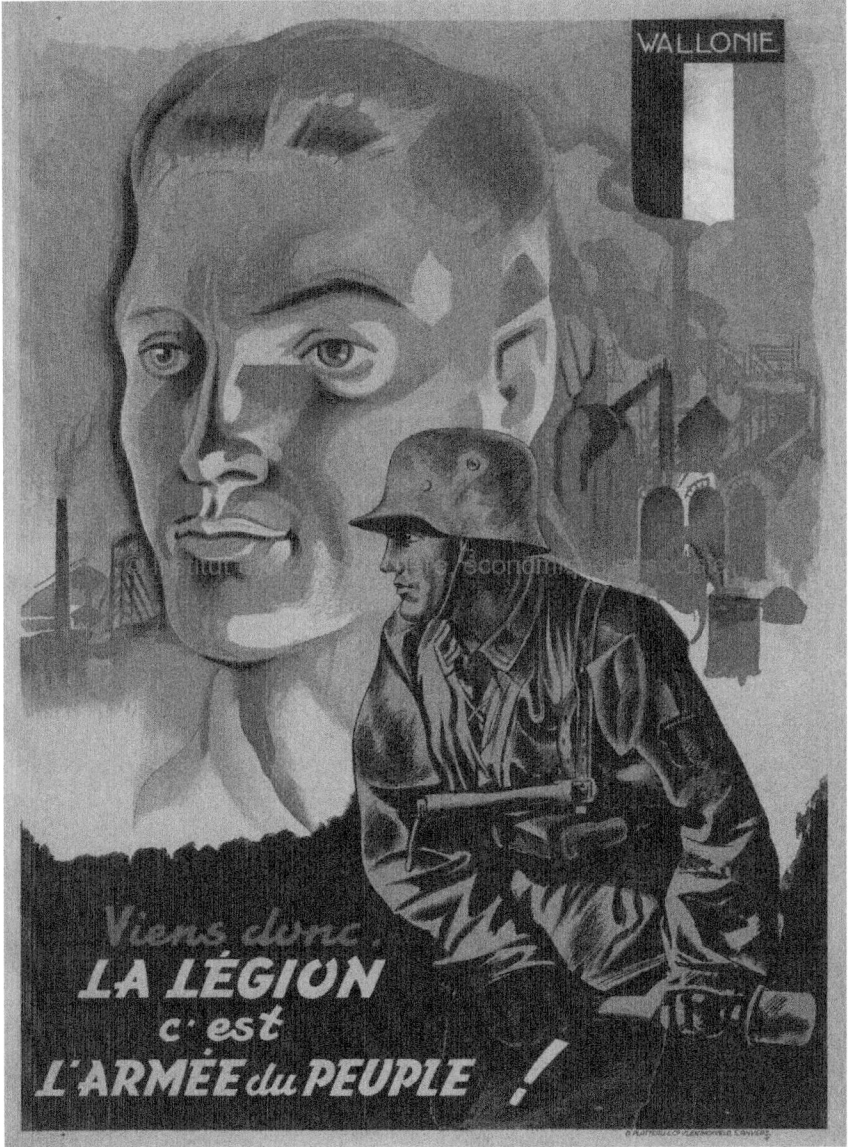

The "Wallonien"

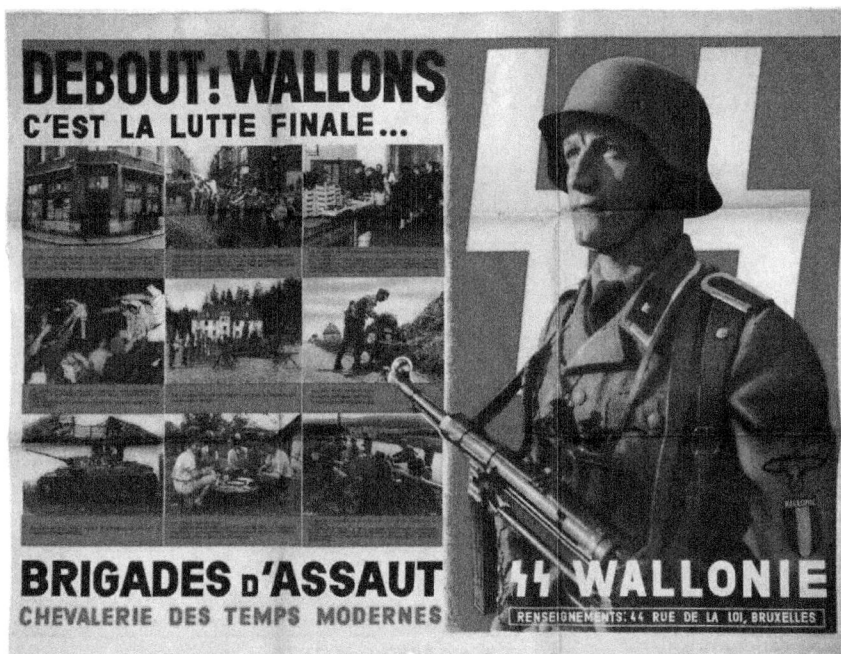

Leon Degrelle distributes cigarettes to his soldiers, Pomerania, late February 1945.

The "Wallonien"

Walloon soldier, Pomerania, 1945.

SS-Untersturmführer Léon Gillis from the Wallonien Division scans for enemy forces in Pomerania. He is armed with a StG 44 assault rifle.

The "Wallonien"

The "Wallonien"

Printed in Great Britain
by Amazon